THE BLACK CANYON
OF THE GUNNISON

THE BLACK CANYON OF THE GUNNISON

A STORY IN STONE

The natural and human history of Black Canyon
of the Gunnison National Monument

John Dolson

PRUETT **P** *PUBLISHING COMPANY*

Boulder, Colorado

First Edition
1   2   3   4   5   6   7   8   9

Printed in the United States of America

Library of Congress Cataloging in Publication Data

Dolson, John, 1949-
   The Black Canyon of the Gunnison.

   Bibliography: p.
   Includes index.
   1. Black Canyon of the Gunnison National Monument
(Colo.—Guide books.   2. Black Canyon of the Gunnison
National Monument (Colo.)—History.   3. Natural
history—Colorado—Black Canyon of the Gunnison
National Monument.   I. Title
F782.B5D64   917.88'19   82-531
ISBN   0-87108-622-0   AACR2 (pbk.)

This book is dedicated to:
my wife, Debbie, for moral support
and
Mrs. Kathleen Koch, for her perseverance
and
my newborn son Josh, whose first outdoor
experience was at Black Canyon.

The Painted Wall and West Elk Mountains, from Warner Point

Preface

The natural history of the Gunnison River Canyon is not unique to the American West. Like the Royal Gorge, Grand Canyon, and others, its history began billions of years ago and was shaped by multitudes of prehistoric environments, animals, and mountain ranges.

Unlike many other more famous canyons, however, its past has remained relatively untalked about, usually understood in some detail only by a handful of park rangers and scientists. This book has been written to help explain some of the more remarkable aspects of the area's geology, environment, and human history. All three of these elements have been intertwined to create the striking features of Black Canyon of the Gunnison National Monument.

Hopefully, this work will enable many others to more fully appreciate the fascinating history of this area.

Acknowledgments

Dr. Richard G. Beidleman has made most of this writing possible through years of painstaking research into the natural history of Black Canyon. His pioneering efforts to develop interpretive themes for the National Park Service have resulted in a unique collection of data concerning the Monument area. His guidance as an inspiring teacher and friend has provided the substance for this book.

Special thanks go to Bob Cruz of Amoco Production company for his help illustrating this book.

Table of Contents

THE BLACK CANYON REGION

Introduction

Few words adequately describe the splendor of Black Canyon of the Gunnison National Monument. Far too many people pass it by. A relative unknown, it ranks among the deepest and narrowest canyons in North America, dwarfing such popular chasms as the Royal Gorge and Bryce Canyon. Sheer walls, shadowed depths, and striking red sunsets produce unique feelings in each visitor.

For most, the canyon is a surprise, even a shock. The 8-mile drive to its rim is uneventful, and no gorge appears even after entering Park boundaries. Suddenly, the yawning chasm at Tomichi Point unveils a glimpse of a strikingly different canyon.

Perhaps the Utes were the first to describe it accurately, "Tomichi," the Ute name for the Gunnison River, roughly translates to "land of high cliffs and plenty water." Somehow though, this description is insufficient. Black Canyon is not "just another canyon"; it is unique in many ways.

While its walls are steep, they are also very close together. It is very long, almost 100 miles, of which the most spectacular 22 lie within the National Monument. The canyon is geologically unusual and exposes some of the oldest rocks in the world. Indians and early settlers avoided its forbidden depths.

The Narrows overlook, North Rim

At the narrows, a view seen completely only from the North Rim, Black Canyon is a precipitous 1,750 feet deep, 1,100 feet wide, and only 40 feet across at the bottom. Few canyons so dramatically combine length, depth, and width. In some sections, daylight lasts only a few hours, quickly replaced by perpetual shadow.

Wildlife abounds on both rims, and the Gunnison River offers excellent fishing. Surrounding mountains and valleys are rich in human history and unique geology.

To truly appreciate Black Canyon, stop and sit for a while. Listen to the sounds of the inner gorge and look closely for its secrets. Sit silently and become a part of the muted roar of the Gunnison River far below, or watch eagles soaring effortlessly atop powerful canyon updrafts. If time permits, drive the 110 miles to the North side, barely 1,000 feet away. Each rim offers different views.

But remember, please obey park regulations and help keep Black Canyon scenic for future generations.

1
The
Rocks

The geologic story of Black Canyon is the story of an imprisoned river, a river trapped on a rising mountain block with nowhere to go but down. This is the story of superposition, one often repeated throughout the West. The figures on pages 5 and 6 illustrate the evolution of the canyon.

Approximately 2 million years ago, the Gunnison River slowly twisted and meandered over a flat, featureless plain. Slowly, over countless centuries, forces generated deep within the earth lifted this plain upward. Where weaknesses existed, the rocks cracked and sheared past one another, forming huge faults. The mountain of Vernal Mesa began to grow.

In the nearby West Elk Mountains, volcanic outbreaks piled millions of tons of hot debris into the Gunnison River. Alternating layers of volcanic ash built sturdy cliffs along both banks of the river. Swelled by meltwater from nearby ice age glaciers in the San Juan Mountains, the Gunnison slowly sawed into the hard rocks of its newly formed prison.

To the west, free of confining walls, the tiny Uncompahgre River sliced easily through the soft Mancos Shale. Millions of years later, the Uncompahgre would outcarve the larger Gunnison, forming a broad gentle valley.

As the Gunnison cut deeper, it penetrated successively older layers of rock. Slowly, wind and water relentlessly stripped away the cliffs of confining ash. Too

Rocks and Age

350 my
Pennsylvanian
Weber Fm.
deposited in
adjacent areas.

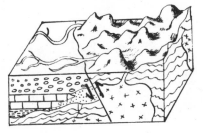

Events

Renewed uplift
Birth of
Ancestral
Rockies.

600 my - 350 my
Cambrian thru Miss.
No rock
record remains.

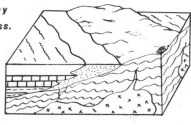

Erosion, seaway
invades
nearby areas.

1.1 - 2.2 Billion years

Precambrian
Schists, gneisses
and granites form.

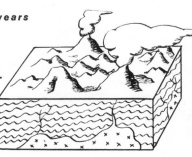

Metamorphism
and mountain
building
forms canyon
core.

2.2 billion years.

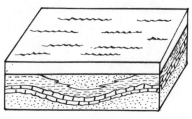

Sediments
deposited in
subsiding
seaway.

Canyon Geologic History

Rocks and Age

Events

60 my to present. Tertiary volcanics and Ice Age gravels cap rim.

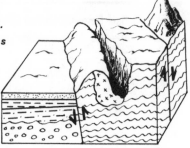

Repeated uplift, erosion and volcanism trap the Gunnison on Vernal Mesa. Canyon Forms.

105 my - 60 my Cretaceous Mesa Verde Group deposited nearby.

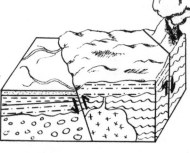

Renewed uplift, seas retreat.

170 my -105 my Cretaceous Dakota and Mancos Fms. form.

Shallow seaway invades the area.

350 my - 170 my Jurassic Morrison deposited.

Erosion, swamps cover area, dinosaurs flourish.

Canyon Geologic History

late, however, for the Gunnison had begun carving through the oldest and hardest rocks in the rising mountain—the dark granites and schists of the inner gorge.

The deeper it cut, the more the river uncovered the story of the chain of events that preceded the trapping of the Gunnison. These events would combine to determine the shape of the canyon, its biology, and, ultimately, the life of its people.

The complete story has unraveled slowly. Year by year the Gunnison scours its riverbed deeper. Tumbling boulders, grinding gravel, and flood-ravaged silt slice continuously through the resistant rock; two human hairs per year, an inch each century. After 2 million years, the canyon deepened to its present 2,800 feet. The final carving, however, is but part of a larger, more complex picture. The complete geologic story is close to 2 billion years old.

The oldest rocks are those of the inner gorge, the dark metamorphic schists and gneisses. These rocks may have once been sands and gravels squeezed and reformed deep under primeval oceans at the base of a growing mountain chain. Perhaps this mountain chain resembled the Colorado Rockies or the coast ranges of California.

These rocks formed deep within the earth almost 2 billion years ago. In time, they would rise to the surface as countless mountain ranges above them formed, weathered away, and rose again. Today, the inner gorge is all that is left of the core of these ancient and unseen mountain ranges.

During the mountain-building process, molten columns of rock forced their way upward, sometimes erupting as volcanoes. Some of these dikes reached the surface, but many cooled slowly, deep within the developing range. When solid, they became pegmatites, the beautiful pink rock that cuts across the dark schists, sometimes forming unusual "paintings" on the canyon walls.

The mineral feldspar forms the pink color of the pegmatites. Some of these crystals reach 10 feet across and lie in pegmatites several miles long and hundreds of feet wide. Pegmatites also contain large amounts of quartz and mica, the flaky, transparent mineral once used in Isinglass-windowed ovens. Occasionally, the dikes contain precious ores like gold and silver, but not here in the canyon.

The mountain range formed slowly, sealing its pegmatites and dark schists deep within. Slowly, it weathered away. The Appalachian Mountains are in a late stage of a similar erosion cycle today. By the Cambrian period, 600 million years ago, the high mountains were probably entirely gone.

Almost a billion years of geologic history are lost at this point. Few rocks remain to help decipher the geologic story. However, bits and pieces of this long time period can be studied by examining rocks from surrounding areas.

Sandstones and limestones preserved nearby suggest that few living things sought land as their home during much of this interval. Primitive armor-plated fishes swam strange primeval oceans—probably not near the Black Canyon area, but possibly as close as Colorado Springs where limestones hold their remains. If oceans covered the canyon area at this time, the record of this has been destroyed by erosion. During this interval, the Paleozoic Era came and passed without leaving a trace at Black Canyon. The Appalachians grew, eroded, and rose again during this time period. California did not exist as we know it today. Dragonflies evolved 2-foot wingspans, dominating lands where birds did not yet exist. In the East, huge coal beds developed and thickened in Pennsylvania and Kentucky. Slowly, time wore on.

Three hundred and fifty million years ago another mountain range grew in Colorado. Its rocks, like today's Rocky Mountains, were those of the core of the first range that formed the schists and pegmatites hundreds of millions of years earlier. Tumbling mountain cataracts and eternal winds ground away at the mountains, leaving the massive pebble-studded conglomerates of the Pennsylvanian Hermosa, Weber, and Maroon formations. The record of these ranges is recorded in surrounding mountain valleys but, however, not at Black Canyon.

During the Triassic period, deserts slowly replaced the crumbling mountains, but no record of these lie atop Black Canyon. In Colorado National Monument, only 70 miles north, huge fossilized sand dunes form the beautiful red cliffs of the 200-million-year-old Wingate Sandstone. No record of the Wingate or any other desert-like rock exists at Black Canyon.

What was the area like during this time? Perhaps it formed a stable highland around which the land shifted and changed. Perhaps vast oceans and mountains alternately covered and uncovered it, and the rock record was merely stripped away. We may never know for sure, for the rocks of the inner gorge are over a billion years old while those that cap it are less than 200 million.

Time gaps such as these are termed unconformities. The unconformity at Black Canyon is one of the greatest in the western United States. Thousands of feet of rock and millions of years of time preserved in surrounding areas are simply not present in the National Monument.

About 140 million years ago, deposits from streams and rivers finally left a sliver of rock atop the canyon known as the Entrada Formation. This sandstone is much thinner at Black Canyon than it is at Colorado National Monument, which it caps. To the east, the Entrada is absent, and the younger Morrison Formation caps the dark rocks of the inner gorge. This suggests that the monument area was a subtle highland and that rocks were being deposited and buried along its flanks. Gradually, the dark schists and pink pegmatites were completely covered by these formations.

The great unconformity: the canyon's flat top formed 350 million years ago after erosion of the ancestral Rockies

The resulting unconformity is easily visible today. It forms the remarkably flat top of the dark inner gorge. This flat top is the remnant of the gentle highland that formed from erosion of the mountain ranges of the Pre-Cambrian and Paleozoic eras. The hills of the North Rim are the sedimentary rocks that capped this erosion surface when it was finally buried in Jurassic time.

During the Triassic period, Colorado's climate had been primarily desert, and vast sand dunes covered the state. During the Jurassic, however, Colorado's climate shifted from desert to humid lowland. Lush swamps of the Morrison Formation engulfed and eventually covered the highland. Broad-leafed plants and huge dinosaurs covered the lush terrain. To the west, the growing Sierra Nevadas explosively made their appearance, scattering clouds of volcanic ash across the western United States.

Rivers, flowing from distant snow-capped volcanoes, laid down the red and white shales and sandstones of the Morrison Formation. Dinosaurs, floundering in ancient swamps and sluggish rivers, left their bones scattered throughout the red and white rocks. No dinosaur skeletons have yet been found at Black Canyon, but

Narrow side canyons form along ancient joint sets such as this one near Dragon Point

the Morrison Formation has yielded hundreds of these bones at Dinosaur National Monument, 150 miles to the northwest. It is very possible that dinosaur skeletons exist within park boundaries. The bones could be in the hills of the North Rim or the red and white rock layers lining the road along the entrance to the monument on the South Rim.

Imperceptibly, the land changed. A new formation, the Dakota, formed atop the Morrison as a shallow seaway invaded the area. Slow-moving deltas, giant soaring reptiles, and nearby oceans mark the age of the Dakota Sandstone. Its beaches and river deltas held sands and muds ground fine from hundreds of miles of transport. These well-rounded sands would one day trap important sources of ground water and petroleum. Today, the Dakota caps the hills of the North Rim.

During the Cretaceous period, about 80 million years ago, growing mountain chains to the west caused the canyon area to sink. Imperceptibly, a broad, shallow seaway crossed North America. In the Black Canyon region, ocean muds settled slowly, forming the soft, white shales of the Mancos Formation. The Mancos was long ago eroded from the rim of the canyon, but shapes the white "adobe hills" near Montrose, Colorado.

For 20 million years, the muds of the Mancos Shale accumulated beneath the shallow seaway. Swimming reptiles and strange fish lived and died in the warm waters. Two-inch sharks shared waters with 60-foot swimming dinosaurs.

The shale, rich in alkali, supports few plants and turns into a sticky, gooey clay when wet. Many people call this type of terrain "badlands," as it closely resembles the Badlands of South Dakota. Today, shells of extinct mollusks and abundant fossil fish are common in the Mancos Shale.

About 60 million years ago, the land began swelling upward as new mountain ranges rose to the west and east. Once again, the deeply buried schists and granites that would some day line the inner gorge were slowly shoved upward along newly developing faults. As the land rose, the seaway drained back to its present location in the Gulf of Mexico and the Arctic Coast. The dinosaurs became extinct and mammals triumphed. Two-foot-high horses hid in dense underbrush, and birds completely replaced the flying reptiles. Thick coals developed to the north and west in swamps that replaced the Mancos Ocean.

Over the next 60 million years, the land changed into many different forms. A series of mountain ranges formed and disappeared. Volcanic outbreaks in the West Elks and San Juans sputtered violently off and on for 40 million years, leaving rugged ranges in their wake. Gold and silver deposits formed near the volcanoes, as did rich deposits of zinc, lead, and molybdenum.

Two million years ago, at the end of the Teriary period, the Ice Age clutched Colorado. Wooly mammoths and saber-toothed tigers roamed a frozen land not yet inhabited by man.

Meltwater from huge mountain glaciers poured into the lower valleys, swelling the Gunnison River. Flowing across a featureless plain, the Gunnison was quite unlike its modern form. No cliffs bound its banks, and frequent floods often shifted the location of the riverbed completely.

Only a few chapters in earth history remain to update the canyon's geologic story. Again, the land rose across the ancient fault zones. New volcanic outbreaks trapped the river, and the canyon began forming. Such incidents are not unusual,

Chasm View. The river is 100 feet below

but the unique shape of the canyon, extremely deep and narrow, owes itself to a combination of circumstances.

First, the Gunnison is a large river, fourth in size in Colorado. It drops rapidly through the Monument—an average of 95 feet per mile. At one point, from Pulpit Rock overlook to Chasm View, the river plunges an incredible 180 feet in a half mile. Compare this gradient with that of the Colorado River in Grand Canyon (7.5 feet per mile) or the Mississippi River near the Gulf Coast (16 inches per mile). This unusually steep gradient, formed by a sharp tilting along the Red Rocks fault zone, gives the Gunnison a powerful cutting ability.

Second, few side streams join the Gunnison as it flows through the Black Canyon. Normally, tributaries help carve wide canyons as they wear down the sides of existing gorges. At Black Canyon, however, the Gunnison is the only significant canyon-carver.

Pulpit Rock, South Rim

Third, the rocks of the inner canyon are exceptionally hard and not easily eroded. They are more easily cut down vertically than they are eroded outward.

Thus, a combination of rapid down cutting, little side cutting, and resistant rocks made for a very narrow and deep canyon—"one of the narrowest and deepest in the world."

Gradually, time and earth forces would shape the land into its present form. The volcanic outbreaks ceased 1 million years ago, and the huge glaciers retreated to isolated mountain valleys. The climate warmed, and the wooly mammoth became extinct. Primitive Folsom men moved into the Colorado Rockies. More advanced tribes arrived later and in turn were driven out of Colorado by the onrush of civilization.

The canyon formed slowly. The process continues. What does the future hold? Who can tell? More downcutting and more widening is certain, but will the mountains continue to rise, or will they slowly erode? How long will the canyon exist—how deep will it become? No one can tell. Of this, one can be certain—the canyon will be here for many years to come.

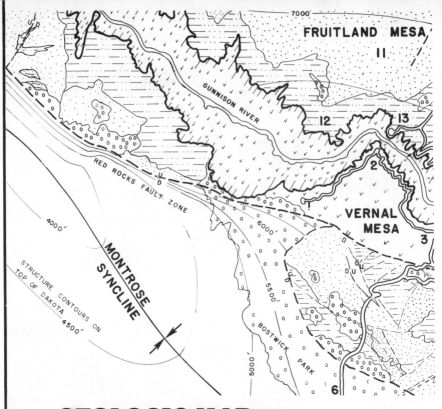

GEOLOGIC MAP:
BLACK CANYON AND VICINITY

(REVISED FROM U.S.G.S. MAP 1-584 BY WALLACE HANSEN, 1971)

SCALE
| 1/2 0 1 2 3 |
MILES
| .5 0 1 2 3 |
KILOMETERS

POINTS OF INTEREST
1. High point
2. Chasm view
3. Gunnison Point Visitor Center
4. Campground and ranger station
5. River portal road
6. South rim road
7. Gunnison tunnel
8. Crystal Dam & Nat. rec. area
9. Morrow Point Dam & Nat. rec. area
10. North rim road
11. Site of 1879 forest fire
12. Highest cliff in Colorado
13. North rim campground
14. The Narrows
15. North rim ranger station

ROCK SYMBOLS

Quaternary Alluvium

Tertiary Volcanics

Cretaceous Mancos Shale

Cretaceuos Dakota Sandstone

Jurassic Morrison
& Entrada Sandstones

Precambrian Granite
& Metamorphics

Approx. Canyon Edge

Fault

14

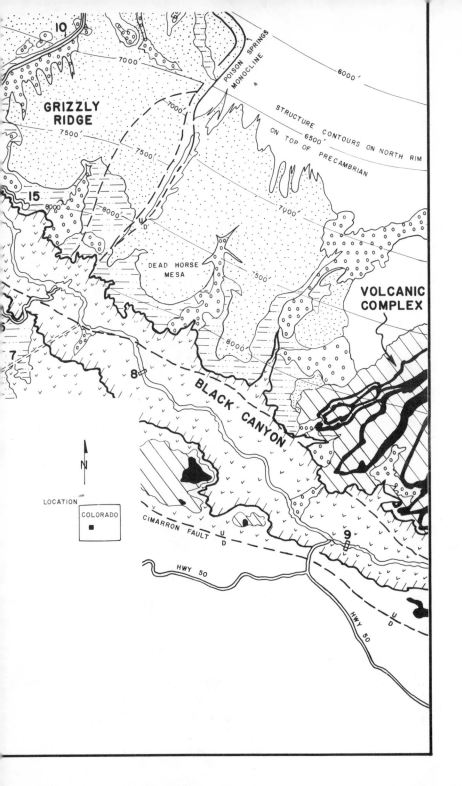

10

GRIZZLY
RIDGE

7000'

7500'

7500'

8000'

8000'

15

POISON SPRINGS MONOCLINE

6000'

STRUCTURE CONTOURS ON NORTH RIM
ON TOP OF PRECAMBRIAN

6500'

7000'

7500'

DEAD HORSE
MESA

8000'

VOLCANIC
COMPLEX

7

8

BLACK CANYON

N

LOCATION

COLORADO

CIMARRON FAULT   U
                  D

9

HWY 50

HWY 50

U
D

2
The
Environment

Winds blow gently over Black Canyon from the southwest. As they rise from the valleys 2,000 feet below, temperatures drop and rain falls. In July, short, violent thunderstorms are more common, often bringing scattered lightning strikes and small fires. September's rain mists gently down, hanging for hours in drifting fog banks. Throughout winter, snow accumulates, falling in wet sheets by October, melting by June.

For most of the year, however, the rains pass over the canyon, falling on surrounding mountain ranges. The higher the elevation, the lower the temperatures and the greater the chance for rain. Low-lying Montrose bakes in a scant 10 inches of rain yearly. Black Canyon, 2,000 feet higher, picks up a bare 15 to 25 inches. The rugged San Juans, higher still, bathe in 40 to 70 inches annually..

In the West, water shapes most life forms. Its presence or absence controls entire living communities. Few other factors control the canyon's environment like water. With only 20 inches falling yearly, the canyon's inhabitants need special adaptations for survival. Along the rim, the scrubby brushland is best suited to these conditions.

THE BRUSHLAND. To the unfamiliar eye, it often presents a ragged, scraggly

Serviceberry

appearance. Trees are uncommon, a straight passage difficult. No other Colorado habitat resembles it. To those who know it, it is a world of darting birds, rugged plants, graceful deer, and occasionally, hunting mountain lions.

The brushland is built for survival. Every plant and animal has a place and a purpose. Short trees and plants need very little water. Compare the stunted brushland of Black Canyon with the lush forests of Olympic National Park, where 250 inches of rain fall annually. Few of Olympic's plants could survive the comparative drought of Black Canyon.

Other factors help control the brushland's appearance. At 8,000 feet, winter temperatures can plummet to 30°F below zero. Spring arrives in mid-June and winter begins in September, making a short growing season.

The plants grow only as close together as the available water allows. Many plants have special water-conserving adaptations. The needles of the prickly pear cactus save water by slowing evaporation. Gambel oak leaves have a waxy coating to preserve their precious water content. Spiny yuccas send long taproots deep in search of water.

Animals must adapt also. Buried in rock potholes, eggs of tiny insects and crustaceans await enough water to allow their hatching. For example, fairy shrimp eggs hatch only when dissolved minerals indicate the water will not dry up before the adult shrimp have a chance to lay a new generation of eggs. Larger animals like ground squirrels can store water in fat cells through long periods of drought.

Gambel Oak

Other plants and animals are less sensitive to the environment, drifting in and out of the brushland and living in a variety of habitats. Some organisms are more common than others and tend to dominate the environment. Here in the brushland, the serviceberry, Gambel oaks, and mountain mahogany bushes are most common.

The serviceberry, a member of the rose family, is a large bush often covered by small, hard red berries resembling miniature apples. Aptly named, it services many animals, notably sleek mule deer and nervous chipmunks.

The berry has a bitter taste, but was once an important food source for wandering tribes of Ute Indians. The industrious Utes ground its juices into a pulp of deer meat and fat, drying the mixture in strips. Pemmican, the final product, made an excellent food staple during lean winter months.

The Gambel oak owes its name to Bill Gambel, a pioneer botanist who described it in the 1840's. This miniature oak is one of the American West's most common plants. It is a relative of the giant Eastern oaks, but seldom grows over 20 feet high, limited in size by the scant rainfall.

The Gambel oak's tiny acorns and tender leaves nourish numerous animals. Its dense thickets are unusual; each small tree is connected to the next by an intertwined root system. During fires, the roots sprout dozens of new trees, increasing the size of the thickets and helping to reclaim the charred land. The South Rim's dense oak forests may be due in part to old lightning strikes or brushland fires set by Ute hunting parties trying to drive out small game.

Mountain mahogany bushes lie scattered atop both rims, notably along can-

Mountain Mahogany

---

yon edges. Like all living things in the monument, they are geared for survival. Their feathery seeds twirl gracefully to the ground, slowly expanding and contracting as the moisture levels in the air change. Eventually, these sensitive seeds spiral and twist enough to bury themselves into the rocky soil. If the time and place is right, a new shrub grows where the seed so laboriously planted itself.

Years ago, the Utes made a mahogany-red dye from the plant's root system and used the shrub's branches for arrow shafts. Straightening the crooked green branches took time and patience. Each one had to be continuously pulled through a small hole drilled in an antler or piece of bone until the branch was smooth and perfectly straight.

Many other plants compete for the limited water along the rim. Blooming requires larger amounts of water than usual, so different plants flower at different times, stretching out limited water reserves. In summer months, blue lupines, white daisies, and yellow tansy asters offset the dark canyon walls. In fall, blossoming rabbitbrush brightens the land with its brilliant yellow foliage.

Throughout the year, sagebrush spreads across disturbed areas, old roads, and open meadows. In 1853, Captain John W. Gunnison, while passing around Black Canyon, cursed the pungent sage's sharp aroma. The aroma is the same, but this plant's location shifts with time, helping to stabilize disrupted areas. Fires, roads, and overgrazing cattle are just some of the forces working to reshape the land. When an area is disturbed, the sage quickly moves in, holding the soil in place and trapping precious water. Some call it a bane, others a blessing. In Black Canyon, it blankets old roads and in some places, abandoned corrals.

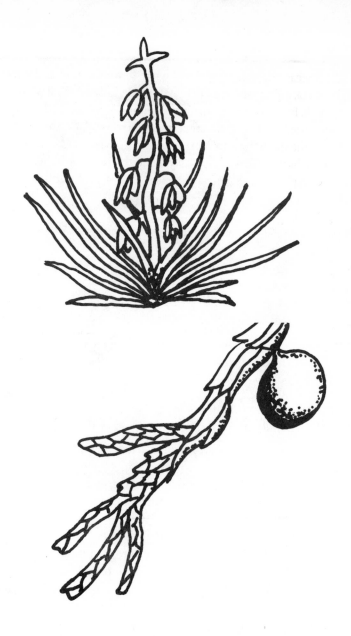

Yucca
Utah Juniper

Along the wetter parts of the monument, thickets of chokecherry shelter young deer and feed hordes of insects. The dark purple berries make a tangy jam and attract numerous birds. Chokecherry thickets are common along streams and ponds, notably near Chasm View.

In dryer areas, the sharp leaves and white flowers of yuccas dot rocky outcrops. The yucca, a lily, maintains a delicate balance with the small white yucca, or pronuba, moth. Each needs the other for survival. The yucca feeds the moth and the moth fertilizes the yucca. No other insect can do this. Neither organism can exist without the other, thus forming a symbiotic relationshp.

In slightly higher regions, especially along the North Rim, well developed forests of pinon pine and Utah juniper trees make a striking contrast to the thick brushland.

The gnarled, twisting trunks of Utah junipers lend a macabre atmostphere to these stunted forests. Many of the trees approach 1,000 years in age. The scraggly bark burns easily, making ideal kindling for flint and steel fires. The bluish berries are bitter tasting but a popular food source for birds.

Small cones and short pine needles identify the pinon pine. Every seven years, if conditions are right, these cones produce a peanut-like seed which was a popular part of the Ute diet. Along Warner Point nature trail, several Ute day camps indicate that the pinons of Black Canyon may once have supported men as well as wild animals.

The pinon-juniper woodland is unique; a product of the dry West. On the South Rim, High Point houses a well-developed stand. The bulk of the vegetation on the North Rim grows amid this type of forest.

Many biologists consider this habitat the best for supporting mule deer. In addition, the pinon forests shelter a unique grasshopper, a species whose wings are yellow on the North Rim and red on the South Rim. Apparently, the great depth of Black Canyon has proven a biological barrier, speeding up evolution in the process.

The canyon's shape causes other aberrations in nature. Along the more gentle slopes, thick forests of Douglas firs cling to rocky crags and cliffs. As in all environments, seemingly small differences in climate can prove enormous ones for living things. Canyon shadows slow evaporation and allow these trees to survive. Along north-facing slopes, temperatures are slightly cooler and moisture lingers even longer. It is here that the Douglas firs are thickest.

These forests harbor few animals other than sleeping porcupines, but allow a multitude of ferns and mosses to thrive beneath their protective canopy. Normally, the firs grow at elevations of 10,000 feet or more in Colorado, but the canyon's shadows and north-facing slopes can simulate the climate common to higher elevations.

In wetter climates, such as coastal Oregon, Douglas firs often grow hundreds of feet high and 10 to 15 feet in diameter. At Black Canyon, however, the meager rainfall holds their size to that allowed by available water levels.

Winter at Gunnison Point *Courtesy of* NPS

As the seasons change, so do the plants and environments. Spring's brilliance fades to a burnt summer green, brightening again in fall. Winter's sharp contrasts of black and white paint yet another picture. No one time is best to visit the monument, as each season has a special significance.

3
The Animals

Black Canyon abounds with wildlife. Different environments along the rims and canyon floor support different collections of plants and animals. These ecosystems not only share some animals, but also shelter some species characteristic only to their unique habitats.

Raccoons, for instance, are common only along the river, while the graceful mule deer roam throughout the monument. Golden Eagles frequent all habitats, but elusive pigmy nuthatches seldom leave the pinon-juniper woodland.

Some animals are active only at specific times, others at no particular hour. Night-loving owls share their limited food supply with hawks, who hunt the same prey while the owls sleep. Likewise, mice are active mainly at night, while chipmunks feed during the day. As always, nature strives for a balance.

A late evening drive often surprises a nocturnal porcupine. These awkward pin cushions are common, especially near pinon pines. Porcupines are rodents. As such, their front teeth, the incisors, never stop growing. Chewing hard bark is a necessity for its survival, since the tree's hard covering continually grinds down the teeth, keeping them a respectable size. If not continually honed, the incisors can grow into the skull, killing the animal.

Contrary to popular belief, the porcupine cannot throw its quills. It can,

Look-alikes: The Colorado Least chipmunk and the Golden-mantled ground squirrel

---

however, painfully slap them into a predator's hide, where they slowly make their way deep into the skin. Be careful if you spot one of these sluggish rodents.

Early morning and evenings are ideal times to locate herds of mule deer. These deer are the only deer species native to the Colorado mountains. In May and June, newborn fawns add an additional touch of beauty to the monument. These tiny creatures weigh less than 2 pounds when born. Only their spotted camouflage protects them, and if surprised, they instantly freeze close to the ground. They have no scent when born, an advantage which often makes the freezing tactic work.

In winter, heavy mountain snows drive large herds of elk into the monument. By June, most of these animals have migrated back to the relative seclusion of their high mountain valleys. Herds of 20 or more are common in winter months.

Throughout the year, numerous bird species frequent Black Canyon. Some, like the bald eagle, are migratory and just passing through. Others, like the swifts and golden eagles, are year-round residents and common sights.

The white-throated swifts are common around overlooks. Flying with them are everpresent violet green-backed swallows. The swallows occasionally rested on protruding branches, but the swifts are almost constantly airborne—even mating for brief moments while still flying. Their sleek black bodies and white bellies identify them as they streak along the canyon edges in search of insects at speeds of up to 200 miles per hour. Watch the swifts lock wings and fall like twirling helicopter blades as they mate briefly in midair.

Several pairs of golden eagles nest in the canyon, where strong updrafts, high

24

cliffs, and ample food make an ideal habitat. Mature eagles have a wingspan of 4 to 6 feet and glide with smooth steady motions with wings held straight. Contrast this with the flight of the turkey vulture, easily mistaken for an eagle, with its jerky, unsteady flight and "V" shaped wing position.

For an excellent chance of spotting eagles, try the Warner Point nature trail anytime from 6:00 a.m. to 10:00 a.m. Look for them soaring upwards on columns of hot air along hills and ridges.

In the evening, find a secluded trail or overlook and listen to the sounds of the canyon's residents.

Sharp, yipping cries usually mark hunting coyote bands. Shrill chirpings probably belong to chipmunks upset by your intrusion. Rustling leaves might mark the passing of a badger or a striped skunk. Both animals are good ones to steer clear of. Sharp whistling cries often reveal groundhog-like marmots. During the day, these animals sun themselves along exposed rock outcrops, keeping a wary eye out for prowling bobcats or hungry eagles.

Seek out shaded rock ledges and look for the remains of dinners left by bobcats and mountain lions. A slow, alert evening drive is often all that is needed to spot one of these magnificent animals.

In years past, bands of bighorn sheep provided occasional meals for these large cats. Today, pressing crowds and increased development have driven these agile sheep to more remote mountainsides. Perhaps some day they will return, but increasing numbers of visitors and expanded developments threaten to make this unlikely.

More commonly, hordes of chipmunks and ground squirrels now dominate

Mule deer

---

the overlooks and canyon walls, begging for handouts. The chipmunks differ from the ground squirrels by having stripes extending to the ends of their noses. Both animals are forever seeking food for storage in underground homes over the long winter months. Like the porcupines, they are rodents and must chew hard foods in order to wear down their teeth. Please keep this in mind if you decide to toss them an unusual food source.

Black Canyon shelters many types of animals. To see them, slow down, walk a lot, and keep alert. No hunting is allowed at Black Canyon. With proper management, the canyon's residents will be around to delight people for years to come. Morning and evening hours are best for sightings, but a quick eye is equally important. Be patient and alert; the rewards will follow.

Sunset View

Pulpit Rock

Inner canyon from SOB draw

Inner canyon from SOB draw

Sheer walls

The canyon from the North Rim

Fall colors *Courtesy of* NPS

Winter at Warner Point

4
Into the Gorge

Towering cliffs, gentle breezes, dark walls, and blue skies; tumbling cataracts and an ever present roar; all describe the Gunnison River canyon.

Few places project such awesome solitude as the canyon's inner depths. Passage is difficult and limited in some spots to 100 yards. Access is hard in all places and sometimes dangerous.

Scrambling over rocks, through bushes, sliding down steep slopes, and edging down jagged talus blocks, one finally reaches the bottom. The rewards are unforgettable. Evening comes early as the sun rapidly sinks behind sheer cliffs. Flickering campfires create dancing shadows on the dark walls. Solitude and primitive grandeur offset the struggles of getting there.

A night on the bottom leaves a different impression with each individual. To some, the night arrives with a threatening aura of foreboding. To others, the wild rugged canyon brings a soaring sense of independence. No matter what the impression, it is always a lasting one.

Several primitive routes penetrate the gorge. All are difficult. Park rangers register all back-country travelers. A permit is a must, and camping is limited.

On the South Rim, Tomichi Point, Gunnison Point, and Warner Point offer the best access.

Canyon mist, Tomichi Point

Tomichi Point leads to a series of cataracts and falls with about 1 mile of river access along the bottom. Virtually no good beaches line this stretch, so camping is often limited to the smoothest rocks available. The route in is rocky all the way to the bottom and takes 1.5 to 3 hours one way.

Gunnison Point, at the visitor center, is the most popular route and takes about the same time as Tomichi to penetrate one way. River access is limited to about .5 miles, and the canyon is about 2,000 feet deep here. Several sandy beaches line the bottom, and deep pools hold large trout. The water is cold—38°F—and the current is swift.

About one-third of the Gunnison Point route winds along a primitive trail through a Douglas fir forest. The rest of the route cuts across rough talus slopes. Although this route is considered the easiest access, many still have difficulty getting in and out.

Warner Point opens up spectacular vistas of the deepest and wildest part of the monument. Here, the canyon reaches 2,800 feet in depth beneath the towering confines of the Painted Wall, Colorado's highest cliff. About 2 miles of shoreline provide excellent fishing. Sandy beaches are common, and some large rock overhangs give shelter from occasional storms. This is undoubtedly the best camping and fishing area in the monument, but it is extremely difficult and tiring to reach.

When entering Warner Point, check your directions with park rangers carefully—the route is easy to miss and takes 4 to 7 hours to reach the bottom. Several people have been injured or lost on this route due to careless planning. Well-thought-out excursions and care are the best techniques for entering any part of the monument.

The Painted Wall, highest cliff in Colorado

The first portion of the Warner Point route dips up and down along the Warner Point nature trail. Near Post 9 on the self-guided nature trail, the route swings left along another ridge. Stay on the ridge for one-half to three-quarters of a mile. From here, in a large saddle on the ridge, the route plunges straight down amidst a tangle of bushes and large trees, sometimes over slippery springs or around hugh boulders. The last third of the route is comparatively easy, with more open spaces and less scrambling.

The North Rim offers several other routes to the bottom. As on the South Rim, register with the North Rim ranger before entering. The most popular routes are SOB Draw and Long Draw.

Aptly named, SOB draw leads to spectacular scenery at the base of the sheer cliffs of Chasm View and the Painted Wall. About 2.5 miles of river are open to the physically fit along this route. A short walk upstream leads to a good-sized water-fall. Large numbers of pools line the bottom, dammed at each end by 20-foot high boulders jarred loose from the precipitous cliffs.

SOB is basically a rocky, steep access. The upper third heads through some vegetation, which rapidly thins out. Plan on 2 to 4 hours to reach the bottom. The trailhead begins about .5 to .75 miles north of the North Rim campground. This route is the most popular access point for rock climbers seeking to conquer the dangerous Painted Wall.

Long Draw gives a steep, straight route into one of the most impressive parts of the monument—the narrows. Here the powerful Gunnison is driven into a chasm only 40 feet wide at its base. A large, relatively calm pool of water belies the enormous rapids downstream, where the river is unleashed again. The North and South Rims tower 1,750 feet above, separated from each other by only 1,100

29

The Narrows, 40 feet wide, 1,750 feet deep *Courtesy of* NPS

---

feet at the top. At this point, Black Canyon has one of the deepest and narrowest clefts of any canyon in the world.

Long Draw is a short, steep but comparatively straight route into the canyon. Echo Canyon provides a similar access to the narrows from the South Rim. Be sure to register with the North Rim ranger before going in.

Animals and plants of the inner canyon are typical riverbottom inhabitants, although many people have noted the comparative scarcity of many animals in these inaccessible stretches. Mountain maples and small willow thickets are very common.

Fishing at SOB draw

Ringtail cats and raccoons fish nightly along the river and sometimes raid a stringer or two of fish. Black bears have been sighted along the bottom, but are considered rare. Beaver find the Gunnison too powerful to dam, but compromise by building their lodges along the riverside near large, calm pools. Tunnels burrowed as far back as 50 feet give quick entrance and exit to the pools from shore.

Fishing is excellent. Large populations of undisturbed 1- to 2-pound rainbow and brown trout enjoy the relative safety of the secluded Gunnison. The cold river temperatures encourage a unique fighting spirit developed over long generations of unmolested wilderness growth.

Rainbows are more common in the large pools, while the browns seek more turbulent waters near the edge of rapids. Both varieties seem to take virtually any bait, but lures and the time-honored worm are most popular.

When camping along the bottom, camp far enough from the water to allow a 6-foot river rise during the night. Dams upstream cause unexpected river fluctuations. Many a camper has lost equipment by not taking this into consideration. The new Crystal Dam may control this irritating nuisance, but perhaps not. Extra caution is necessary to prevent unpleasant and perhaps tragic events.

In the past, uncontrolled floods often raged through the canyon, sweeping the floor clean of debris, piling huge loads of dead trees high up the steep slopes. While on the bottom, look for the old high-water marks and try to picture the devastating flood scenes that early explorers must have encountered while exploring the hazardous gorge.

Today, most evenings along the Gunnison are idyllic if the fishing is good and the weather dry. The inner canyon is a bad place to be if you decide to camp when the weather fouls or the fishing sours. Try to plan a trip of midsummer or early fall for two or three days. Brief stays hardly allow enough time to recover from the arduous hike in.

The inner gorge is a place of rugged, unparalleled scenery—difficult to reach, hard to forget. Enter and exit it with respect and you will be able to enjoy your stay; Black Canyon's wilderness is not for everyone.

5
The Canyon and Its People

The canyon's earliest human inhabitants may have been Folsom men. Little evidence of these people remains but for a few arrowheads found scattered in the nearby Uncompahgre Valley.

Very little is known of Folsom man's life here, sometime between 10,000 and 20,000 years ago. His life was probably very simple, relying on wild herbs and small game for most food. Occasionally, however, his appetite grew larger, as evidenced by Folsom point arrowheads found embedded in the bones of extinct wooly mammoths and other large Pleistocene animals.

With time, Folsom Indians slowly disappeared from the western United States, either dying out or blending with new, more advanced tribes which migrated south from Asia across the Bering Strait. In any event, 3,000 to 4,000 years ago, the Ute Indians became the dominant tribe in the Rocky Mountains.

The Utes were a short, stocky, dark-skinned race linked by language to the Shoshoni tribes. Utes were nomadic, wandering from camp to camp in search of migrating buffalo and deer. Primarily a hunting society, they used very little agriculture, contrasting sharply with the agrarian Pueblo Indians only 150 miles south of Black Canyon.

The Utes differed from the Pueblo tribe in other ways. While the Pueblos built elaborate stone cities clinging to cliffs and high mesas, the Utes built fragile,

The Painted Wall

brush-covered wickiups. While the Pueblos were peaceful farmers, the Utes were aggressive warriors. When drought and warring neighbors forced the Pueblos to leave their Mesa Verde home in the 1200's, the Utes moved on to new water sources and successfully resisted any attempts to capture Ute land.

By the time white settlers reached Colorado, the Colorado Rockies belonged exclusively to Ute tribes. In the Black Canyon area, two tribes, the Uncompahgre and Tabeguache, controlled the hunting lands. Game in this area was plentiful, especially around the pinon groves to the south, near Ridgeway, Colorado.

Like other Indians, the Utes took full advantage of their terrain and native plants and animals. Summer camps were in cool mountain valleys, winter camps in sheltered lowlands. Ute warriors fashioned 6-foot bows from juniper wood and flint arrowheads from small flint quarries west of Montrose. Mountain mahogany bushes provided arrow shafts, and serviceberry juice helped preserve meat for lean winter months. Hunting bands often drove game into traps or over cliffs, as hunting was done on foot before 1500 A.D.

On Black Canyon's North Rim, some the these old hunting traps may be scattered across the top of the Painted Wall. At Serpent's Point, 2,000-foot high cliffs border a large section of canyon wall on three sides, almost forming an isolated "rock island." A narrow neck 200 feet wide connects this partial island with Fruitland Mesa. Numerous arrowheads and other artifacts have been found here, including what may be the remains of large pits and traps. Possibly, Ute hunters drove deer onto this isolated point and into the pits and primitive traps where hidden hunters butchered them at will. The only way off the point was a plunge over the cliffs or a desperate run at the narrow entrance, either route certainly fatal.

This way of hunting, however, probably declined with the increased use of the horse. Around 1540, Spanish explorers penetrated Colorado, bringing horses with them. The New World had not had horses for more than 1 million years prior to this time. Some of these animals escaped, rapidly multiplied and became large herds of wild mustangs and paints.

The horse soon became the Indian's most prized possession. Horses allowed hunting parties to range long distances from camp and bring in much larger quantities of meat. Plains Indians developed tepees, a primitive form of camper-trailer. When the camps moved on, the poles, wrapped with the tepee, were dragged along by a horse. Any baggage, small children, etc., were piled onto this "travois" and bounced along the prairie to the next camp. Whole villages could pack up and be gone in minutes.

Although the Utes were excellent horsemen, they never fully developed the tepee. Some families continued to use the primitive wickiup for shelter up into the late 1800's. In fact, neighboring tribes like the Arapahoe and Kiowa referred to the Utes as "bad lodge makers." Today, some of the crooked poles used to make these poorly built tepees can still be found standing on the Uncampahgre Plateau west of Montrose.

Ute activity at Black Canyon, however, was apparently limited. The rugged terrain and mysterious depths sprouted many superstitions. Few records exist of Indian activity in the bottom, and only a few sites along the rim show that hunting was done here. Undoubtedly, hunters camped and wandered along both rim tops, but apparently did not venture into the canyon. Indeed, Indian superstitions about the inner gorge were perpetrated by many early settlers who believed no man could enter Black Canyon and return alive.

The first white explorers to reach the Uncompahgre Valley, however, never had a chance to prove this superstition right or wrong. In 1765, a Spanish explorer, Juan DeRivera, wandered in and out of the Uncompahgre Valley near Montrose without ever seeing the canyon. In 1776, Padres Escalante and Dominguez dropped over Dallas Divide south of Montrose and moved north along the Uncompahgre River. They passed within 10 miles of the future National Monument without seeing it.

Escalante was exploring a possible trade route from Old Mexico to California. He made extensive maps and records wherever his expedition went. Along the way, he attempted to Christianize any tribes contacted. The Utes seemed uninterested, but did provide a guide to lead the Spanish over Grand Mesa and through the Grand Junction area into Utah. At no time did these Indians show the padres Black Canyon.

Escalante made the first detailed study of the Black Canyon region, but missed Black Canyon entirely, like many modern travelers. In the late 1700's, however, French trappers undoubtedly became the first white men to gaze into the canyon's depth.

These trappers followed mountain streams and rivers in search of beaver. They were the vanguard of hordes of people soon to follow. Their extensive knowledge of the American West would soon pave the way for less intrepid individuals to follow.

The first recorded visit by a trapper was that of Antoinne Roubidoux. Roubidoux built a trading post near Delta, Colorado, around the 1830's. The Utes burned it to the ground, however, in 1837. Roubidoux and others like him undoubtedly saw Black Canyon, but no one bothered to record the historic moment. The trapping era came and went with no written record of the first sighting.

The trapping industry came to an abrupt end around 1840 as European fashion shifted to new styles. By now, a trickle of settlers had begun moving West, but Colorado remained primitive and wild.

In 1849, however, gold was discovered in California. The rush was on, mostly bypassing the rugged Colorado Rockies through South Pass in Wyoming. Far off the beaten path, Black Canyon remained known only to a handful of individuals. In 1853, the Army Corps of Engineers was to permanently change this.

Burgeoning gold camps needed food, supplies, and people. The railroad offered the quickest solution to the transportation problem. Congress directed the corps to survey the best possible route to the California gold fields. One of these expeditions would pass into, and out of, Black Canyon.

Captain John Williams Gunnison would survey a route through the southern section of Colorado. Gunnison was a young and promising officer. He reached the edge of the Front Range by September, 1853. He crossed his first mountain pass, LeVeta, and entered the broad San Luis Valley. From here he climbed over Chochetopa Pass and down into the present site of Gunnison, Colorado. Here he discovered Tomichi Creek (now the Gunnison River), the river of "high cliffs and plenty water." Gunnison mistook it for the Colorado and plodded westward, cutting a wagon road as he went.

Near what is now Blue Mesa Dam, he entered the first rugged confines of Black Canyon. Passage became increasingly difficult and horses and wagons had to be lowered over cliffs on ropes. Discouraged by the slow and arduous progress, Gunnison climbed out of the canyon and passed completely around its remaining 90-mile length.

He never saw the National Monument area. Nor did he want to, as his survey showed a rail route through even the entrance to this portion of the canyon would be financially impractical, if not impossible.

Pushing north from Montrose, Gunnison hewed his road far into Utah, to the Servier Lake district. Here, while cooking breakfast one morning, he was ambushed and killed by a band of Paiutes. Fifteen other men died with him. Gunnison's death was not in vain, however, as other members of his expedition returned with the valuable records of his survey. Among other things, Gunnison built the first road to the Western Slope. He also determined that a more northerly route for a railroad was best.

Thus the first waves of settlers would pass around Colorado in their search for instant wealth, while the Rockies held more gold and silver than most could envision.

In 1859, discouraged California prospectors struck it rich near Denver, and a new rush was on. The first strikes centered around the eastern ranges, but by the 1870's huge deposits of gold and silver were found in the San Juans, only 35 miles south.

New surveys formed as railroads and settlers pushed into southwestern Colorado. In 1874, the Hayden geological surveys completed the first detailed reconnaissance at Black Canyon.

The Hayden survey skirted the North Rim for most of its 100-mile length, noting rock type, rivers, distant landmarks, and other features. Ferdinand Hayden's surveyors had a zest for detail and accuracy, despite their limited education. Hayden himself, who explored farther north in the Yellowstone region, was known by the Indians as "the white man who picks up rocks while running."

Long View, North Rim

In their search for information, the Hayden team reportedly lowered one of their geologists 1,000 feet into the canyon on a long rope. When he came out, he supposedly confirmed the Indian superstitions by declaring that no man could go farther and still live.

As Colorado grew, so did the canyon's reputation of inaccessibility. Black Canyon remained a barrier to be traveled around, not over or through.

As the Montrose area grew, however, the Denver and Rio Grande Railroad began searching for an easy route to the San Juan mines. The grade through Black Canyon looked good, especially when compared to the steep hills the railroad would have to climb if the canyon were skirted. By 1881, after years of hard work and blasting, the first and only narrow gauge railroad in Black Canyon was completed. Winding beneath spectacular cliffs and along the beautiful Gunnison, the Denver and Rio Grande route became a popular mode of travel through western Colorado. The railroad climbed out of Black Canyon at Cimarron, just upstream from the Monument boundary, as the cost of building the railroad through this section was prohibitive. The steam engine once used in the canyon is now on display at Morrow Point Recreation Area, near Cimarron.

Bypassing Black Canyon from Cimarron and further west was not easy. The grade up Cerro Summit required two engines and was very slow. In 1882, the frustrated Denver and Rio Grande hired Byron H. Bryant to complete a survey of the unknown, "inaccessible," and mysterious section of canyon downstream from the rail terminus.

No one had supposedly ever entered Black Canyon here and lived to tell about it. Indeed, no one had probably ever tried.

The task was formidable. What began as a 20-day trek lengthened into a 65-day nightmare. Supplies ran low, the December temperature plummeted to below zero, and most of the daylight time involved just getting from one miserable place to the next. Very little surveying could be done each day. Each morning, the surveyors climbed into the rugged canyon from the top. At night they climbed back out to the base camp 2,000 feet above.

The river was only partially frozen and very dangerous to cross. Somehow, by March, the survey was completed. The verdict: a rail route through this section would be highly impractical, if not impossible. The canyon remained impassable. The railroad could not enter the last 30 miles, and no one had succeeded in passing through its entire length without climbing back out.

As the San Juan gold fields developed, farmers and merchants settled the fertile, but parched Uncompahgre Valley. Food, so desperately needed in the mining communities, was scarce and expensive. Local farms were limited to flood-prone patches along the small Uncompahgre River. Farmers looked with longing to the much-needed water in the Gunnison River, but Black Canyon completely prevented any tapping of this ideal irrigation source.

Enterprising farmers diverted a portion of the Uncompahgre for irrigation. The Uncompahgre, however, was too small to do much good. A larger source was badly needed.

While most settlers glumly accepted their fate, a persistent "dreamer" spawned a novel, but "impractical" idea. The "dreamer," a Frenchman named

Will Torrence surveying near the Narrows, 1901 *Courtesy of* NPS

Lauzon, envisioned a tunnel through Vernal Mesa to divert a portion of the Gunnison for irrigation. Most people thought the idea absurd. After all, the tunnel would have to penetrate 9 miles of solid granite with pinpoint accuracy, a very difficult and expensive task. Besides, virtually nothing was known of the inner gorge downstream from the rail station at Cimarron. Passage through it from here on was impossible. Lauzon was persuasive, however, and soon had a loyal and dedicated following. By 1900, his followers were exerting considerable political pressure.

The Colorado Senate studied the idea but needed more information. Where was the best tunnel site? What problems must be overcome? How much would it cost? These questions had to be answered before anything else could be done. Optimistic for the first time in years, eager residents quickly outfitted a new survey team.

The plan was simple, but the canyon complex. Leading the expedition was William W. Torrence, superintendent of the Montrose Power and Light Company. Four other men joined him in the attempt.

Torrence planned to travel exclusively by river in two large wooden boats, similar to those used by John Wesley Powell in his exploration of the Colorado River in 1869. The group would start at the end of the rail line at Cimarron and travel the 30 miles to Delta, Colorado in four to five days, completing a detailed survey as they went. The river promised a change in plans.

It was September, 1900. Even before entering the present section of the monument, the rapids grew dangerously swift. After one day, they had traveled less than 1 mile. The next day, the main boat sank, destroying all provisions and survey equipment.

Undaunted, they pushed deeper into the gorge. New supplies were brought down from the rim September 25. They decided to continue, counting on three or four more days to finish.

Foot by treacherous foot, the canyon deepened. Dark walls rose vertically thousands of feet. A feeling of gloom slowly settled over the crew. Turning around became increasingly difficult, then impossible. No route out presented itself. Escape meant moving forward into increasingly dangerous terrain. After three weeks, the tired, hungry, and cold adventurers had traveled less than half way, only 14 miles. Backup teams on the rim lost sight of the team and considered the surveyors doomed.

It seemed impossible for the situation to worsen, but it did. Rounding a corner near Rock Point overlook, they saw the canyon narrow to only 60 feet. Waterfalls and cascades blocked further travel downstream. Huge 60 foot boulders prevented passage around the rapids. If they were to live, they must climb out.

Desperate and hungry, the discouraged and frightened surveyors started up the steep walls of the North Rim. They probably chose a route near the present location of the Narrows, just upstream.

Later investigations would show that no route at this point was easy or safe. Some passageways were almost vertical and loose rock threatened everyone. At some points, the men had to inch up narrow chimneys 1,500 vertical feet above the rapids. Near the top, one of the men had to be talked out of jumping into the river to his death. Finally, after 12 exhausting hours, they reached the safety of the North Rim, still 15 miles of wilderness away from the nearest ranch.

Looking back down into the canyon, they eyed the churning white water that had stopped further progress. After naming these rapids, the "Falls of Sorrow," they began the 110-mile trek back to Montrose.

For Torrence, failure to complete the survey ignited a fierce determination to return. The other members of the crew would never again attempt to run the monument's rapids, apparently content to agree with Indian superstition.

Public pressure for a tunnel grew, as Torrence and others persuaded Congress that diversion was possible, albeit difficult. In the summer of 1901, the U.S. Reclamation Service sent a hydrographer, A. L. Fellows, to see how accurate these claims were.

Will Torrence   *A. L. Fellows*

Will Torrence and A.L. Fellows, pioneer canyon surveyors, 1902 *Courtesy of* NPS

Torrence and Fellows hit it off immediately and began preparing for a new survey. Torrence would not make the same mistakes twice.

The unyielding wooden boats were replaced by durable and flexible air mattresses built with watertight compartments for storing gear. They planned to stay out of the river as much as possible, portaging back and forth from the south and north banks if necessary.

They left August 12, 1901, from Cimarron. After a few days, fresh supplies reached them near the present site of Crystal Dam. Resupplied, they pushed on. No real problems ensued until reaching the "Falls of Sorrow," where Torrence had been forced out of the canyon a year before.

Canyon whitewater

Again, no route around or through the rapids looked possible. Undaunted, they tossed their gear into the foaming river and jumped in after it. For a few terrifying seconds, they bounced and slid down the river landing exhausted but alive on some rocks in midstream. Like before, they could not turn back, and the route ahead was becoming even more difficult.

Gigantic boulders, ground incredibly smooth, made passage difficult. At the Narrows, they drifted slowly along the south bank in the deep 40-foot wide channel. Along the North Rim only a few feet away, a swift current could easily catch them, smashing them against piles of logs and rocks.

At some points, the boulders completely jammed the river, driving it into raging caverns beneath them.

Once, when these boulders completely blocked passage downstream, Torrence and Fellows solemnly said goodbye to each other and plunged into the swirling waters. The river drove them both under the dam and out, unharmed to the other side. Hysterically hugging one another, they reportedly shouted, "Who says Black Canyon is impassable?"

They ran out of food. Hungry and weak, the desperate men somehow cornered a mountain goat and Torrence clung fiercely to it while Fellows killed it. The goat meat would give them the strength to carry on.

The hazards were real. Each turn of the river brought new surprises. No detailed maps or complex gear aided them. Finally, after nine exhausting days, they completed the survey and began the climb out somewhere near Red Rock Canyon, well past the present Monument boundary.

They had done what no men had done before. After 30 miles, innumerable hazards, and 72 river crossings, they had beaten Black Canyon. Even today, few people have managed to do the same, even though the Gunnison River is considerably smaller in volume due to damming upstream of the monument.

The survey was a landmark in Western history. Fellow's notes would prove a diversion project possible. Appropriations for funds would soon follow, and the greening of the dry Uncompahgre Valley would permanently change the way of life in this portion of western Colorado.

The Torrence and Fellows expedition marked the start of the Gunnison River Diversion Project, one of the Bureau of Reclamation's first projects.

Building the tunnel was not easy. The 9-mile bore penetrated dense rock, poisonous gas pockets, stifling heat, and scalding hot springs. The first bore started in 1903 and the final penetration took another 6 years. The entire project, complete with irrigation canals, would cost 7 million dollars and take until 1923 to complete.

Two towns grew up on either side of the ridge separating Montrose from the Gunnison in Black Canyon. In the bottom of Black Canyon, near the present site of Crystal Dam, the town of East Portal grew to house the miners boring west. Near the present intersection of Highway 348 and 50, the town of Cedar Creek housed the drilling teams boring through the mountain to East Portal. Over such a great distance, even small mistakes in calculations could cause the two tunnels to miss one another somewhere deep underground.

Compounding this problem were numerous geological hazards. Part of the tunnel drove through weak, slumping Mancos Shale, where special tunneling techniques were required. Nevertheless, several men died in tragic cave-ins.

While pushing ever deeper toward the granite core, the miners drove into combustible pockets of gas and were forced to flee and later sink expensive and deep ventilation shafts for safety. Deeper still, they penetrated the age-old Red Rock fault zone. Pressures here created high temperatures and drillers never knew when they would cut into a subterranean stream of scalding water.

Gunnison tunnel outlet, near Highway 50

Machinery, crude by today's standards, frequently broke down. Power was supplied by steam plants located at both tunnel entrances. No trains or trucks shipped in extra equipment and men.

To reach East Portal, men and gear zigzagged down a narrow and incredibly steep road. Horse-drawn wagons had to be slowed by dragging large trees under the wheels. This road, now much improved, is the entrance to Crystal Dam.

Spring rains sometimes flooded the tunnel, further delaying work. Work continued year-round, and the men had to contend with bitter winters and the isolation of the inner canyon.

Somehow, by September 23, 1909, the tunnel was officially opened. President Taft personally opened the tunnel amidst gala celebrations. Today, the Gunnison tunnel still provides most of the water used for irrigation in the Uncompahgre Valley.

While most irrigation projects require huge dams, the Gunnison tunnel required only a small spillway. The spectacular environment of the inner gorge remained essentially unchanged. Today, further reclamation attempts meet with much controversy. Three dams, Blue Mesa, Morrow Point, and Crystal, have dammed over two-thirds of the 100-mile-long Black Canyon. Further projects threaten development of lands out of the National Monument boundary downstream and along the North Rim. Without National Monument and Wilderness status, the inner gorge would undoubtedly have been fully developed long ago. The formation of Black Canyon National Monument, however, was almost totally the work of one man—the Reverend Mark Warner.

Sunset View, South Rim

The Reverend Warner realized the canyon's potential for park use as early as the 1920's. While other groups sought to exploit its beauty, Reverend Warner actively lobbied for National Park status. In 1925, some Montrose residents decided to build a toll bridge at Chasm View, creating a bridge even higher than the one at Royal Gorge. Their plan failed, however, as they did not have the money to even build a road into the monument.

While projects like this started and quickly died, Reverend Warner slowly gained support for his idea. Finally, President Hoover created Black Canyon of the Gunnison National Monument in 1933, one of his last acts in office. The park was idle for many years, until a road was built to the rim in the 1940's. Even then, rains often made passage difficult or impossible along the muddy highway.

Today, a paved highway makes travel in and out of Black Canyon simple. The inner gorge has been designated as Wilderness area, and over 300,000 people visit the canyon yearly.

Under National Park guidance, the monument area will remain wild and undeveloped for future generations to see. Undoubtedly, without this protection, no primitive areas would long remain. Hopefully, future generations can come here and gaze upon the canyon's depths and experience the same emotions felt by the Utes, Antoinne Roubidoux, the Hayden surveyors, and W. W. Torrence.

You can help. Remember the Park Service motto when visiting National Parks: "Please take only pictures, leave only footsteps."

6

Black Canyon Road Guide

To use the guide, start at Tomichi Point on Highway 347 and drive through the monument. Match your car's odometer settings with those in the monument.

ODOMETER

0.0   Tomichi Point. The distant flat-topped skyline to the southeast (left in photo) is volcanic rock deposited over the mountain of Vernal Mesa. The hard volcanic rocks helped trap the Gunnison River in its present location.

0.2   STOP. Gunnison Point Overlook and Visitor Center. The overlook is built out onto a 1.1-billion-year-old pegmatite dike. These once-molten sheets of rock formed many miles underground and took years to cool. They are harder than the soft schists and gneisses on either side and thus weather more slowly, eventually ending up jutting into the gorge.

The major shrubbery is Gambel oaks and serviceberry bushes, with some scattered mountain mahogany bushes dotting the cliffsides. Below the overlook a well-developed Douglas fir forest clings to steep slopes. This overlook has a relatively easy access to the bottom. Information on inner-canyon travel can be obtained at the Visitor Center.

TOP: Tomichi Point BOTTOM: Pegmatite dikes cutting metamorphic rock across from Gunnison Point.

0.8 Look for the different rock colors of the inner gorge. The pink streaks are pegmatite dikes. The dark rocks are metamorphic gneisses and schists.

1.1 Note the flat top of the inner gorge. About 400 million years ago, the rocks of the inner gorge formed the core of a huge mountain range. Rivers eroded the mountain range, leveling it to a flat plain. The unusually flat top of the canyon is the remnant of that plain. Later rock formations covered this sur-

TOP: Rounded Pleistocene gravels capping South Rim BOTTOM: Chasm View Overlook, North Rim

face as new environments developed over the long geologic period before the canyon's formation.

1.5 The hills of the North Rim are sedimentary rocks of the Morrison and Dakota sandstones. These hills are covered with a well-developed pinon-juniper woodland, while the South Rim has primarily a thick cover of brushland. Slightly different climatic conditions make this possible.

2.0 Pulpit Rock Overlook and the Rim House. Souvenirs and light meals are sold here. The overlook has excellent views upstream of the camping area along the Gunnison River.

2.2 A well-developed pegmatite dike cross-cutting metamorphic gneiss. Along the overlooks, search for pink feldspar crystals in these dikes as well as quartz and flaky mica.

2.6 Cross Fissures Overlook. Across from this overlook, W. W. Torrence and his four companions made their desperate climb out of the canyon in 1900. The Falls of Sorrow are 1,800 feet below, but not visible.

2.8 Rock Point Overlook. To the right is Echo Canyon, named by Reverend Mark Warner. This man was primarily responsible for obtaining National Park Service status for Black Canyon in 1933. The steep draw leads to the Narrows, where the canyon is 1,750 feet deep, 1,000 feet wide at the top, and only 40 feet wide at the bottom.

2.9 Devil's Overlook. Huge "rock islands" at the end of this overlook seem to reach out for the North Rim, only 1,000 feet away. The small birds flocking around this point are white-throated swifts and violet-green-backed swallows. They seldom rest, spending the bulk of their life in the air. The islands are formed by weathering of huge joint sets that formed when these rocks were strained and cracked during the mountain-building process.

3.1 The rounded gravels on both sides of the road were left by the Gunnison River 2 million years ago before it began carving Black Canyon. Look in the gravels for pebbles of volcanic rock deposited as the Gunnison stripped its confining volcanic veneer off the mountain.

3.4 To the left is a natural spring, one of the few spots of running water on the South Rim. This is an excellent location to look for deer and other animals at dawn or dusk.

3.9 STOP. Chasm View. The North Rim is only 1,300 feet away, but the canyon floor is 1,800 feet below. Looking right, or upstream, you can see a series of waterfalls, some of which are more than 15 feet high. On some days, it is possible to talk to people on the North Rim. The rock you stand on is a large, granite-like intrusion called a Quartz Monzonite, which formed at great depths during the Precambrian.

4.0 Painted Wall Overlook. Across the canyon is a bare spot on Fruitland Mesa caused by an 1879 forest fire. This area has still not recovered fully. The Painted Wall is the highest cliff in Colorado, 2,426 feet high.

4.3 Across the canyon is Serpent Point, capped by yellowish sedimentary rocks of the Entrada Formation. The contact between the basal Entrada and the pre-Cambrian schists is one of the biggest unconformities in the western United States. Ute Indian deer traps have been found near this point.

4.4 Cedar Point and a self-guided nature trail. Cedar Point has an outstanding view of the Painted Wall.

4.7 Dragon Point. Here another excellent view of the Painted Wall offers breath-taking drop-offs and unusual side canyons. Look for the "dragon's head" formed by pink pegmatite dikes crossing the middle of the Painted Wall.

5.3 The distant flat top of Grand Mesa should appear to the north (your right) soon. Watch for deer.

6.4 Sunset View. Grand Mesa, the U.S.'s highest flat-topped mountain rises in the distance, about 50 miles north. The top is a 500-foot thick series of lava flows formed during Colorado's last volcanic outbreaks, 1 to 2 million years ago.

The canyon begins to widen out here as its unusually rapid descent begins to slacken from 100 feet per mile to a mere 35 feet per mile. Where the river flows most slowly, the canyon is widest, as side streams success-fully compete with the Gunnison's ability to carve the canyon deeper. The light-colored rocks in the distance are the tilted and faulted sedimentary rocks of Red Rocks Canyon. Aptly named, Sunset Point is a spectacular area to photograph sunsets, usually a brilliant red.

6.8 The oak-serviceberry brushland is gradually changing to pinon-juniper woodland from here on. Scars on the gnarled pinon pines are caused by hungry porcupines. This mixing of ecosystems allows for abundant wildlife.

7.2 High Point and the Warner Point Nature Trail. The self-guided nature trail traverses the canyon rim for .6 miles to Warner Point, the highest spot on the South Rim. It passes through three major plant groups and offers outstanding vistas of the San Juan Mountains (south) and the West Elk Mountains (east).

Golden eagles frequent this area in the early morning. The mixing of

Morrison Formation

pinon-juniper woodland, brushland, and Douglas fir forest draws an exceptional number of birds, best viewed around sunrise. The larger trees here are over 700 years old.

ODOMETER—The return trip starts back at Tomichi Point and continues along Highway 347 to Highway 40.

0.0 Tomichi Point. The Gunnison tunnel entrance begins shortly upstream. The 9-mile tunnel was completed in 1909 and diverts a portion of the Gunnison for irrigation.

0.4 The Uncompahgre Valley is on the distant right. This valley was carved out of soft Mancos Shale by the small Uncompahgre River. Although the Gunnison is much larger, the bottom of Black Canyon is higher than the Uncompahgre, a fact attributed to the extremely hard rocks of the inner gorge.

0.9 Campground turnoff to the left. The large draw to the right lies atop the shattered rocks of the Red Rocks fault zone, one of the faults largely responsible for the forming of Black Canyon. Here, enormous pressures long ago shifted thousands of feet of rock upward, forming the mountain of Vernal Mesa. As the rock rose, the Gunnison slowly cut downward, forming the canyon.

1.1 River Portal Road. This road goes to the bottom of the canyon and to the Crystal Recreational area. The road is steep and narrow and not suitable for trailers.

1.2 Crossing the Red Rocks Fault.

1.5 Cattle guard.

1.6   Salt Wash and Brushy Basin members of the Morrison Formation are on the right. In some parts of the West, the Morrison yields well-preserved dinosaur bones, such as in Dinosaur National Monument and Escalante Canyon, only 150 and 35 miles northwest, respectively.

2.2   San Juan Mountains, 35 miles south. This range is highly complex, exceptionally beautiful and studded with ghost towns and extinct, deeply eroded volcanoes. Rich silver, lead, gold, and zinc mines remove ores deposited in the cores of these volcanoes.

2.4   Across Highway 50 is Cedar Park, the flat plateau used for farming. The flat surface was formed by a river flowing into Black Canyon during the Ice Age. Over time, other rivers to the west cut into this river's streambed, diverting its waters to the Uncompahgre Valley. This process of river capturing is known as stream piracy.

2.6   Second cattle guard.

2.9   S-curve. Pinon-juniper woodland on both sides of the road.

3.2   Morrison Formation to the right. Shattered rocks are caused by local faulting.

3.6   Third cattle guard.

4.3   Pinon Springs Fault on right. Note the gullies that form along the weakened rocks of the fault zone.

4.5   Rock layers to the right are studded with flint and chert pebbles once used by Ute Indians to fashion arrowheads.

5.0   Crossing the Cimarron Fault. The farmland below (Bostwick Park) lies atop Pleistocene stream gravels eroded into the Mancos Shale.

5.6   Taking a sharp right and heading downhill.

5.8   To the right is a small waterfall flowing past an old landslide where the cliff broke and slid forward.

5.9   Note how the vegetation thins as the white Mancos Shale thickens. Few plants can grow successfully in its alkaline soil.

6.1   Stream gravels on the right were deposited by rivers active during the Ice Age.

7.0   Intersection of Highways 50 and 347. The surrounding hills are layers of Mancos Shale, formally mud on the bottom of a Cretaceous Period ocean.

End of field trip.

7
Bibliography

Beidleman, R. G., *Black Canyon Themes*, 1959. Unpublished compilation of pertinent interpretive information for Black Canyon of the Gunnison National Monument.

Chapman, Arthur, *Watering the Uncompahgre Valley*, 1909. Review of Reviews 40(2):177-182.

Hansen, W. R., 1971. *Geologic Map of the Black Canyon of the Gunnison River and Vicinity, Western Colorado*, U.S.G.S. Map 1-584.

Hansen, W. R., 1971. *The Black Canyon of the Gunnison*, Today and Yesterday, U.S.G.S. Bulletin 1191.

Hunter, J. F., 1925. *Pre-Cambrian Rocks of Gunnison River*, Colorado, U.S.G.S. Bulletin 777:88-91.

Jocknick, Sidney, 1913.*Early Days on the Western Slope of Colorado*, Denver: Carson-Harper Co., 384 pp.

Rockwell, Wilson, 1956. *The Utes: A Forgotten People*, Denver: Sage Books, 307 pp.

Root, George A., 1932. *Gunnison in the Early Eighties*, Colo. Mag. 9(6):201-213.

Shaw, John Henry, 1909. *Exploring the Black Canyon of the Gunnison River*, World Today 17(5):1139-1148.

Weimer, R. J. and J. D. Haun, editors, 1960. *Guide to the Geology of Colorado*, Vol. II, G.S.A., R.M.A.G. 4, CSC.

Index